UNLOCKING THE SECRETS OF ONLINE SALES:A STEP-BY-STEP GUIDE TO BOOSTING YOUR REVENUE

Iris J. McConnell

CHAPTER ONE

INTRODUCTION

There was a small business owner named Anna who had a brick-and-mortar store in her town. She sold handmade jewellery and accessories, and although she had a loyal customer base, Anna was struggling to increase her sales and grow her business.

One day, Anna decided to explore the world of online sales and started researching the best strategies for success in the digital marketplace. She learned about the importance of knowing her target audience and conducting market research, so she spent hours studying her potential customers and learning about their interests and preferences.

Next, Anna focused on building a strong online presence, starting with a user-friendly website that showcased her products and offered an easy and secure online shopping experience. She also made social media accounts for her business and began posting regularly, engaging with customers and promoting her products.

Anna knew that effective marketing was important for success in online sales, so she invested in targeted advertising campaigns, email marketing, and social media marketing to reach potential customers and build brand recognition.

But Anna also knew that providing excellent customer service was important for building a positive reputation and ensuring customer loyalty. She made sure to offer fast and reliable shipping, easy and secure payment choices, and a helpful and

responsive   customer
service team.

As Anna continued to
apply these strategies,
her online sales began to
soar. She was attracting
new customers from all
over the world, and her
revenue grew beyond
what she had ever
thought possible.

Anna realised that
unlocking the secrets of
online sales was a
step-by-step process that
required dedication and
persistence, but the
benefits were well worth
the effort. She had
turned her small business
into a thriving
e-commerce store, and
she knew that she had
only scratched the
surface of what was

possible in the world of online sales.

With a newfound sense of confidence and determination, Anna continued to refine her strategies and explore new chances for growth, confident that she could achieve even greater success in the years to come.

As Anna's experience demonstrates, uncovering the secrets of internet sales necessitates a step-by-step approach as well as a commitment to learning and progress. There's always more to learn about the world of e-commerce and digital marketing, whether you're a tiny business owner like Anna or a major organisation.

If you want to increase your internet sales and earnings, I recommend you act now. Begin by learning about your target market, developing a strong web presence, and adopting successful marketing methods. Remember to prioritize offering exceptional customer service and establishing a positive customer experience.

You, too, can achieve success in the realm of internet sales if you use the appropriate tactics and are prepared to learn and adapt. So why not take the first step today and start your road to discovering the secrets

of online sales? Grab
your copy today.

WHY ARE ONLINE SALES IMPORTANT?

Online sales are
becoming more and
more significant in the
modern economy, and
many companies have
realized the potential of
the online market for
extending their
consumer base,
generating sales, and
attaining long-term
growth. The following
are some of the factors
that make online sales so
crucial:

1. **Global Reach**: By
utilizing online sales,
companies may connect
with clients on a global
scale, overcoming

geographical and linguistic boundaries. Businesses can reach potential clients in other cities, states, or even foreign nations by using a website and online store to extend beyond their neighbourhood.

2. Online sales are always available, day or night, regardless of the hour. In other words, shoppers don't have to worry about store hours or big lines because they can shop whenever they want from the convenience of their homes.

3.**Economical**:
Businesses may find it economical to increase their sales and earnings by engaging in online sales. Businesses can

save money while also expanding their customer base and income because of fewer overhead expenses and the ability to automate many parts of the sales process.

4. **Personalization**: Businesses can customize their marketing and sales strategies by using online sales to target individual customers with offers and messaging that are based on their interests and purchasing patterns. In the long run, this can help companies cultivate deeper connections with their clients and boost client loyalty.

5. **Data analysis**: Online sales offer companies useful information and insights that can be used to enhance their marketing and sales strategy. Businesses can decide how to best maximize their online presence and increase their revenue by looking at measures such as website traffic, consumer behaviour, and other metrics.

Online sales are practical for both customers and enterprises. Customers may purchase from anywhere, at any time, without leaving their homes, while businesses can manage their sales and inventory from a single location, free from the hassles of running a physical store.

Online sales are, in general, a crucial component of the contemporary corporate environment. They give companies the chance to expand their consumer base, boost sales, and experience long-term growth, all while giving customers convenience, customization, and access to a greater variety of goods and services. Whether you own a little business or a major organization, investing in online sales is essential to maintaining your competitiveness in today's digital economy.
data.

HOW MIGHT THIS GUIDE HELP YOU INCREASE YOUR REVENUE?

If you're new to online sales or want to improve the performance of your current online store, "Unlocking The Secrets of Online Sales", can help you get there. Here are a few ideas to help you raise your revenue:

1. **Comprehensive and Simple to Follow**: This book takes you step by step through the process of setting up and maintaining an online store. The material is presented clearly and concisely, making it simple

for readers to understand.

2. **Covers All Areas of Online Sales**: This tutorial covers all areas of online sales, from establishing an online business to maintaining consumers. This provides readers with a thorough understanding of what it takes to succeed in internet sales.

3. **Emphasizes Revenue Growth**: The major purpose of this guide is to assist readers in increasing their revenue. The information offered is intended to assist

businesses in increasing sales and revenue.

4. **Provides real Tips and methods**: The guide provides organizations with real tips and methods for increasing online sales. These pointers are based on tried-and-true strategies that have helped other firms flourish in e-commerce.

DIFFERENT TYPES OF ONLINE SALES MODELS

There are various sorts of internet sales models, each with its own set of advantages and disadvantages. The most frequent models are as follows:

1. Business-to-consumer (B2C) sales entail selling to individual customers. The most prevalent sort of online sales is business-to-consumer (B2C) sales, which are employed by a wide range of organizations, from small e-commerce startups to major multinational corporations.

2. B2B (business-to-business) sales entail

selling to other businesses. B2B sales might be more complicated than B2C sales since they frequently include contract negotiations and managing long-term customer relationships.

3. Direct-to-consumer (D2C) sales entail avoiding middlemen and selling directly to customers. D2C sales are growing in popularity because they provide businesses with more control over their sales and marketing tactics.

4. Dropshipping is the practice of selling things that are shipped straight from the manufacturer or distributor to the client, with no involvement from the seller. Dropshipping can be a low-risk approach for new online retailers to get started because it requires no upfront inventory investment.

5. Subscription-based sales entail selling things or services regularly, such as a monthly subscription box or a software-as-a-serv

ice (SaaS) offering. Subscription-based sales can provide a consistent revenue stream for online vendors, but they can also necessitate a significant amount of continuous maintenance and support.

COMMON CHALLENGES WITH ONLINE SALES

Online sales provide numerous chances for organizations to broaden their reach and increase income. However, as with any business, there are drawbacks to online sales. Here are some of the most common issues that businesses face when selling online:

1. **Competition**:
   Online sales may be fiercely competitive, and standing out in a crowded marketplace can be tough. Businesses must develop ways to distinguish themselves from their competitors and attract clients.

2. **Trust**: Trust is vital in any commercial transaction, but it can be more difficult to create trust online. Customers may be apprehensive to buy from a new or unfamiliar online company, especially if they have had negative experiences in the past.

3. **Shipping and fulfilment**: For online firms, shipping and fulfilment can be a logistical headache. Businesses must ensure that their shipping processes are dependable and that orders are delivered on time and in acceptable shape.

4. **Payment processing**:
   Another crucial part of Internet sales is payment processing. Businesses must select a secure and dependable payment processor and ensure that their clients' payment information is secure.

5. **Customer service**: Building a loyal customer base requires excellent customer service, which can be difficult to give in an online situation. Businesses must respond quickly to customer enquiries and complaints, and their websites must give clear and helpful information.

6. **Technical issues:** Online sales necessitate a dependable and user-friendly website or e-commerce platform. Website unavailability or sluggish load times can have a detrimental impact on sales and customer satisfaction.

7. **Online fraud**: Businesses that sell online face the risk of online fraud. Businesses must take precautions to protect their customers' personal and payment information, as well as monitor for fraudulent activities.

Overall, while there are challenges to online sales, businesses that can overcome these challenges while also providing a positive customer experience can reap significant benefits from selling online.

CHAPTER TWO

SETTING THE STAGE FOR ONLINE SALES

Setting the stage is critical to your success in online sales. You can attract and keep clients, increase income, and develop a sustainable business by laying a solid foundation for your e-commerce firm. Here are three critical steps to preparing for online sales:

1. **Recognize your target audience and their needs**.

Understanding your target demographic and their demands is the first step in preparing for online sales. Who are your ideal clients? What are their problems and obstacles? What makes them want to buy something?

Understanding your target demographic allows you to adjust your marketing messages and product offerings to their wants and needs.

2. Developing an enticing value proposition

After you've identified your target audience, you'll need to develop a compelling value proposition. A value proposition is a statement that communicates to your customers the unique benefits and value that your products or services provided. Your value proposition should be clear and succinct, and it should distinguish your company from its competition. A solid value offer can assist you in attracting and retaining customers, as well as increasing sales and revenue.

3. Establishing quantifiable objectives for your online sales

Finally, it is critical to establish measurable goals for your online sales. What do you hope to achieve with your e-commerce venture? Do you want to boost your revenue, gain more clients, or improve your conversion rate? Whatever your objectives are, it is critical to define precise, measurable, attainable, relevant, and time-bound (SMART) objectives. This will allow you to track your progress and make changes as needed.

CHAPTER THREE

SETTING UP YOUR ONLINE STORE

Setting up an online business can be a daunting undertaking, but with the correct tools and direction, it can be a pretty simple process. In this chapter, we will look at the essential tasks involved in creating an online store, such as selecting the correct e-commerce platform, designing your storefront, adding goods and product descriptions, and configuring payment and delivery options.

Choosing the Best E-commerce Platform

The first step in creating an online business is selecting the appropriate e-commerce platform. There are numerous e-commerce platforms accessible, each with its own set of features and pricing structure. Shopify, WooCommerce, BigCommerce, and Magento are some of the most prominent e-commerce platforms.

When selecting an e-commerce platform, keep your specific needs and budget in mind. Consider the following points:

1. **Ease of use**: Some e-commerce systems are easier to use than others,

especially for beginners. Look for a platform with a user-friendly interface and an intuitive design.

2. **Customization options**: Look for a platform that allows you to personalize your store to match your branding and design choices.

3. **Payment choices**: Make sure the platform supports the payment alternatives you want to give your consumers.

4. **Shipping choices**: Look for a platform that

interfaces with the shipping companies you intend to employ and allows you to configure shipping costs and options.

5. **Customer support**: Look for a platform with solid customer service, as you may require assistance with technical issues or debugging.

Designing Your Storefront

After you've decided on an e-commerce platform, the next step is to design your storefront. Customers will notice your storefront first when they visit your online store, so make a nice first impression.

Consider the following factors when constructing your storefront:

1. **Branding**: Make sure your shop reflects your business identity, including your logo, colour scheme, and typefaces.

2. **Navigation**: Make it easier for customers to find what they're looking for by categorizing and subcategorizing your products.

3. **Visuals**: Use high-quality

product photographs and videos to highlight your products and offer customers a clear idea of what they are purchasing.

4. **Mobile optimization**: Make sure your storefront is mobile-friendly, as many customers will be browsing on their smartphones or tablets.

Adding Products and Product Descriptions

The next stage in creating your online store is to add your products and product descriptions. When adding products, make sure to include the following information:

- Product name: Make sure the product name is descriptive and clear.

- Product Description: Describe the product in detail, including its features, benefits, and specifications.
- ges and videos: Use high-quality images and films to demonstrate the product from various angles and in action.

- Price: Show the product's price, including any

discounts or promotions.

- Inventory: Keep track of your inventory levels to ensure you have enough goods to meet consumer demand.

Setting Up Payment and Shipping Options

The final step in creating an online business is to configure payment and shipping options. Consider the following while creating payment options:

1. Payment gateways: Determine the payment gateways

you want to provide to your customers, such as PayPal, Stripe, or Authorize.net.

2. Payment processing fees: Understand and account for the processing fees associated with each payment gateway in your pricing strategy.

3. Fraud prevention: To limit the risk of fraudulent transactions, implement fraud protection procedures such as address verification and card security codes.

Consider the following while configuring shipment options:

1. **Shipping carriers**: Select your preferred shipping carrier, such as FedEx, UPS, or USPS.

2. Set up shipping charges depending on weight, distance, or a flat fee.

3. **Shipping alternatives**: Provide many shipping options, such as standard, expedited, or overnight delivery.

CHAPTER FOUR

DRIVING TRAFFIC TO YOUR ONLINE STORE.

Driving traffic to your online business is crucial in the realm of e-commerce for boosting sales and attaining long-term growth. Businesses may increase website traffic and customer acquisition with the correct approaches and techniques, increasing sales and establishing a solid online presence.

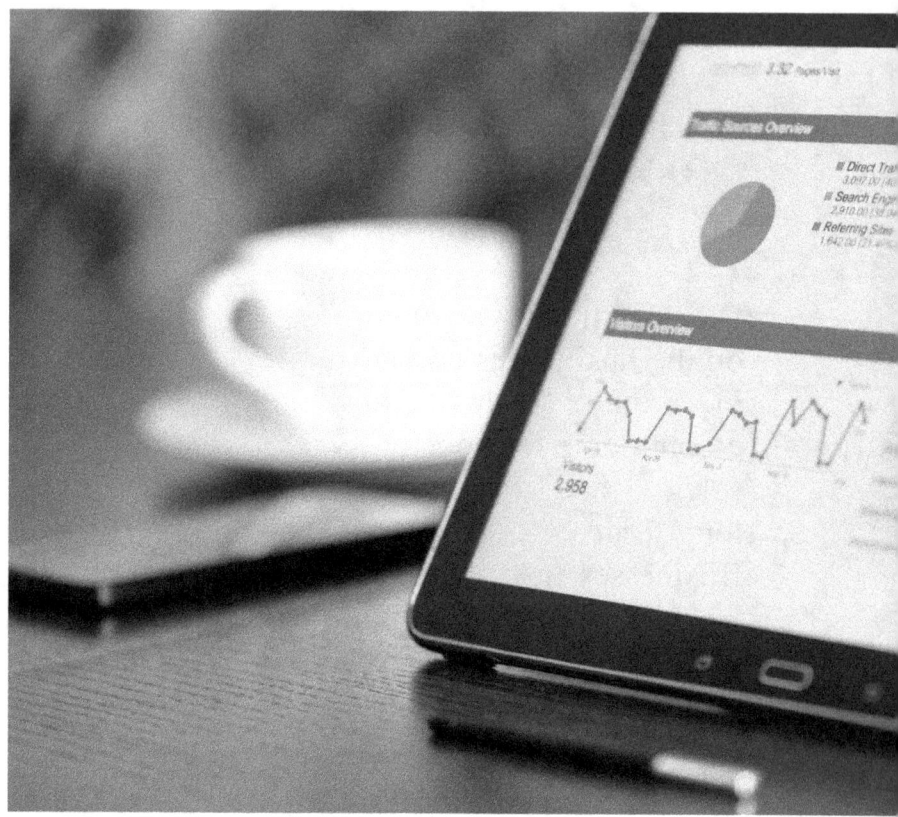

. The following advice may help you increase visitors to your online store:

CREATING A CONTENT STRATEGY

One of the most successful strategies to generate visitors to your online store is to build a content plan. This requires providing valuable and entertaining content that resonates with your target audience and motivates them to visit your store.

Some examples of content that you can generate include:

1. **Blog articles**: Write blog entries on topics relating to your products or industry. This can assist establish your store as a reliable source of

information and attract people who are interested in your products.

2. **Social media posts**: Share product photographs, videos, and other engaging content on social media channels like Facebook, Instagram, and Twitter. This can assist boost your reach and attract new followers that are interested in your products.

3. **Videos**: Create product videos, tutorials, and other videos that highlight your products and

provide value to your audience. This can assist enhance interaction and generate visitors to your store.

OPTIMIZING YOUR WEBSITE FOR SEARCH ENGINES

Another key method for boosting visitors to your online store is to optimize your website for search engines. This involves making sure your website is structured and built in a way that makes it easy for search engines to crawl and index your pages.

Some significant tactics for optimizing your website for search engines include:

- Conducting keyword research: Identify the keywords and phrases that your target audience is searching for and incorporate them into your website content.

- Optimizing your website structure: Use clear and descriptive page titles and headers, and make sure your website is easy to browse.

- **Creating high-quality content:** Create content that is valuable and entertaining to your audience, and make sure to incorporate your target keywords in your content.
- **Building backlinks: Build high-quality** backlinks to your website from other trustworthy websites in your sector. This can assist enhance your search engine results and attract visitors to your store.

RUNNING PAID ADVERTISING CAMPAIGNS

Paid advertising can be an effective way to drive traffic to your online store. This involves paying for advertising on platforms like Google Ads, Facebook Ads, or Instagram Ads, to promote your products to a targeted audience.

When running paid advertising campaigns, consider the following:

1. **Targeting**: Make sure to target your ads to a specific audience that is likely to be interested in your products.

2. **Ad copy and images**: Use persuasive ad copy and high-quality images that showcase your products and encourage viewers to click on your ad.

3. **Budgeting**: Set a budget for your advertising campaigns and monitor your performance regularly to ensure you are getting a good return on investment.

BUILDING AN EMAIL LIST

Email marketing can be a powerful tool for driving traffic to your online store and building customer relationships. This involves building an email list of subscribers who are interested in your products and sending them targeted emails with special promotions, new product releases, or other valuable content.

When building an email list, consider the following:

1. **Offering incentives**: Offer an incentive, such as a discount or gift, in exchange for subscribing to your email list.

2. **Creating valuable content**: Send your subscribers valuable and engaging content that is relevant to their interests and provides value.

3. **Segmentation**: Segment your email list based on your subscribers' interests and behaviour, and send them targeted emails that are tailored to their needs.

By implementing these strategies, you can drive more traffic to your online store and increase your revenue.

CHAPTER FIVE

IMPROVE CONVERSION

Maximizing conversions is vital to your success as an online store owner. The amount of website visitors that carry out a desired activity, like making a purchase or filling out a form, is referred to as a conversion. You may boost your sales and accomplish your business objectives by putting conversion rate optimization (CRO) ideas into reality, enhancing the speed and functionality of your website, and minimizing cart abandonment. This is how:

1. Putting Conversion Rate Optimization (CRO) Strategies Into Practice

The concept of optimizing the user experience, content, and design of your website is known as conversion rate optimization (CRO). Optimizing your website for conversions requires running A/B testing, monitoring user behaviour, and making data-driven decisions. You may increase sales and raise your website's conversion rate by putting CRO ideas into effect.

2. Increasing The Performance And Speed Of Your Website

For websites to improve conversions,
performance and speed are crucial components. Your odds of making a sale can be diminished by users leaving your website because of slow loading times. Consider picture optimization, file compression, and the usage of a content delivery network (CDN) to boost the speed and usefulness of your website. These ways can make your website load more rapidly and improve user experience.

3. Decreasing abandoned carts

Cart desertion is a problem that many online store owners confront. Consider putting strategies like complimentary shipping, guest checkout options, and abandoned cart emails into practice to minimize cart abandonment. You may enhance your conversion rate and recover lost sales by employing these tactics.

Any business that wants to maximize its online sales and revenue must focus on improving conversion rates. If your website is receiving a lot of traffic but has a low conversion rate, your marketing efforts are not being maximized. Here are some recommendations for boosting the conversion rates on your website:

- **Make Your Website User-Friendly**: Your website needs to be simple to use and navigate. This calls for ensuring that your website works quickly, is responsive to mobile devices and has a clean, uncomplicated appearance.
Ensure that your website's layout is simple and that people can locate what they're looking for with ease.

- **Make Use of High-Quality Photos and Videos**: Using photos and videos of the greatest quality will enable you to promote your goods and services. To present your things in the best possible way, use high-resolution images and videos. This can help establish customer confidence in your company and drive site visitors to make a purchase.

- Offer Social Proof is a critical aspect of any effective

conversion strategy. This features testimonials, ratings, reviews, and case studies from delighted clients. Social proof can encourage clients to buy from you by developing brand trust.

- **Simplify the Checkout Process**: The checkout method ought to be as simple and streamlined as possible. Reduce the number of steps needed to complete a purchase while keeping a safe and reliable website.

- **Provide Free Delivery and Returns**: Providing free delivery and return is a wonderful way to enhance conversion rates. Customers are more motivated to acquire a product if they are aware that they can return it for a refund if they are displeased.

- Utilizing a sense of urgency and scarcity can help motivate visitors to make a purchase. To evoke a sense of urgency and scarcity, use words like "limited-time offer" and "only a few left in stock."

- **Use personalisation**: Increasing conversion rates through personalisation is a good method. Utilize visitor behaviour and preference data to tailor the content and marketing messages on your website. Engagement and conversion rates may rise as a result.

- **Use A/B testing**: A/B testing is a powerful way for enhancing conversion on your website. Examine the performance of various website components, such as headlines, photos, and calls to action. You can utilize this to determine the components that perform the best and increase your website's conversion rate.

- **Use live chat**: Live chat can help you enhance conversion rates. It enables users to ask questions and obtain rapid responses, which can boost conversion rates and develop client trust in your firm.

- Provide Information That Is Clear and cConcise

  Increasing conversion rates need clear information and Concisecise. Ensure that your marketing materials and product descriptions are simple to grasp and include all the facts buyers require to complete a purchase.

CHAPTER SIX

RETAINING CUSTOMERS AND ENCOURAGING REPEAT SALES

Customer retention and encouraging repeat transactions are critical for the success of any online business. By keeping your existing customers satisfied and incentivizing them to make repeat purchases, you may build your client base and revenue over time. Here are some simple yet effective strategies for customer retention and repeat sales:

- **Provide Excellent Customer Service**: When it comes to customer retention, exceptional customer service is essential. Make sure your customer service team is responsive, helpful, and friendly, and that you can resolve any issues or concerns that your customers may have quickly.

- **Provide Rewards and Discounts**: Loyalty programs are an excellent way to encourage repeat purchases. Offer rewards and discounts to customers who make repeat purchases or refer new customers to your business. This can inspire clients to continue doing business with you and spread the word about your brand.

- **Personalize Your Communications**: Sending personalized emails and messages to your customers can help build a stronger relationship with them and encourage repeat sales. Personalize your communications and recommend products based on their previous purchases and behaviour.

- **Provide Value-Added Services**: Value-added services, such as free consultations or product demos, can help build trust in your brand and encourage repeat sales. Offer these services to your customers as a way to add value to their purchases and demonstrate your expertise in your industry.

- **Implement Special Promotions**: Implementing special promotions, such as limited-time discounts or free shipping, can help encourage repeat sales. Send these incentives to your current clients to thank them for their business and to entice them to make another purchase.

- **Request Feedback**: Requesting feedback from your clients will help you uncover areas where you can enhance your products or services while also demonstrating that you value their input. Use this feedback to improve your product and address any concerns your customers may have.

- **Use Retargeting Ads**: Retargeting ads are a great way to keep your brand top of mind and encourage repeat sales. Use data from previous purchases and behaviour to present advertising for things that your customers are likely to be interested in.

- **Provide Excellent Product Quality**: Providing excellent product quality is essential for retaining customers and encouraging repeat sales. Make sure that your products are of high quality and that they meet or exceed your customers' expectations.

- **Stay Engaged on Social Media**: Staying engaged on social media is essential for building a strong relationship with your customers and encouraging repeat sales. Use social media to display your items, provide helpful suggestions and advice, and communicate with your customers.

- **Make it Easy to Repurchase**: Making it easy for customers to repurchase from you is essential for encouraging repeat sales. Use tools like subscription services or auto-renewals to make it easy for customers to continue purchasing from you without having to go through the entire checkout process each time.

CHAPTER SEVEN

ANALYZING YOUR ONLINE SALES DATA

Analyzing your online sales data is vital for understanding how your business is operating and discovering chances for development. By collecting key indicators and analyzing patterns over time, you can make data-driven decisions that enhance your business and promote development.

SETTING UP GOOGLE ANALYTICS

Setting up Google Analytics is the first step in analyzing your online sales data. Tracking website traffic, user behaviour, and other important metrics is free with Google Analytics. You may learn a lot about how visitors are interacting with your website and where there may be room for improvement by setting up Google Analytics.

Take into account the following advice when configuring Google Analytics:

- **Put the tracking code in place**: To begin gathering data, add the Google Analytics tracking code to your website.
- **Create goals**: Create goals in Google Analytics to keep track of particular actions customers do on your website, like buying something or subscribing to your newsletter.
- Track the source of your website visitors with UTM parameters, such as social media or email marketing efforts.

UNDERSTANDING KEY METRICS

After installing Google Analytics, it's critical to comprehend the most crucial metrics you need to monitor. The following are some of the most crucial metrics:

- **Traffic sources**: By knowing where your website's visitors are coming from, you can better your customer acquisition tactics and optimize your marketing initiatives.

- **Conversion rate:** The proportion of visitors to your website who make purchases is known as your conversion rate. You may find out where your website needs to be improved by tracking your conversion rate.
- **The typical order value**: The average amount that customers spend on your website is your average order value. You can find ways to boost income per customer by monitoring your average order value.

- **Customer lifetime value**: The revenue you can anticipate from a single customer throughout their association with your firm is known as customer lifetime value. You can prioritize your customer acquisition and retention efforts by knowing the lifetime worth of each of your customers.

IDENTIFYING OPPORTUNITIES FOR IMPROVEMENT

You can begin to find areas for improvement once you have a solid understanding of your main KPIs. Analyze your data for patterns that point to potential areas for website or marketing campaign optimization. For instance, you might need to enhance your product descriptions or modify your pricing strategy if you see that your conversion rate is poor for a specific product or category.

To find areas for improvement, think about the following advice:

- Employ SegmentationTo divide your data into various client segments or product categories, use segmentation. By doing this, segmentation to spot trends and patterns that are otherwise hidden when looking at your data as a whole.

- **Perform A/B testing**: Use A/B testing to compare several iterations of your website or marketing initiatives. This might assist you in determining the tactics that result in the highest conversion rates.

MAKING DATA-DRIVEN DECISIONS

Finally, it is critical to use your data to make data-driven decisions. Instead of relying on intuition or assumptions, let your statistics lead your decision-making. For instance, if you're thinking about launching a new product or marketing campaign, utilize your data to determine which techniques are most likely to succeed.

Consider the following data-driven decision-making tips:

- **Create a hypothesis**: Create a hypothesis based on your facts and insights before making a choice.
- **Put your hypothesis to the test**: Experiment or analyze data to put your hypothesis to the test.
- **Evaluate the outcomes**: Measure the outcomes of your experiments or analyses to see if your hypothesis was right.

You can enhance your business, create growth, and meet your objectives by analyzing your online sales data and making data-driven decisions.

CHAPTER EIGHT

SCALING YOUR ONLINE SALES.

After you've established a successful online store, the next step is to scale and grow your business. You can scale your online sales by outsourcing and automating your business procedures, extending your product range, exploring new sales channels, and cooperating with influencers and partners, among other things.

OUTSOURCING AND AUTOMATING YOUR BUSINESS PROCESSES

As your company expands, you may find yourself spending more time on administrative tasks and less time on revenue-generating activities. One solution is to outsource or automate your business processes. Consider hiring a virtual assistant or automating duties like order fulfilment, customer support, and inventory management with software.

Expanding Your Product Line

Another approach to increase your online sales is to expand your product line. Consider adding complimentary products to your current product line or venturing into other product categories entirely. Conduct market research and solicit feedback from customers to determine which products are most likely to succeed.

Exploring New Sales Channels

Investigating new sales channels is another strategy to increase your online sales. Think about working with retailers to sell your products in physical stores or thinking about selling your products on online markets like Amazon or eBay. To reach a larger audience, you might also want to think about branching out into international markets.

Collaborating with Influencers and Partners:

Another strategy for growing your online sales is to partner with influencers and other businesses. Think about cooperating with industry influencers to promote your goods on social media or working with other companies to provide bundled goods or services. These kinds of partnerships can expand your audience and increase your revenue.

Consider the following tips for scaling your online sales:

- **Create a growth strategy**: Create a growth strategy that specifies your objectives and the tactics you'll employ to get them.

- **Continuously measure and evaluate your data**: To determine which growth-promoting techniques are most successful, continuously monitor and analyze your data.

- **Be flexible**: Be ready to adjust your plan as

necessary in response to modifications in the market or consumer behaviour.

You may scale your online sales and achieve long-term success by outsourcing and automating your business procedures, growing your product range, investigating new sales channels, and working with partners and influencers.

CHAPTER NINE

STAYING UP-TO-DATE WITH THE LATEST TRENDS AND BEST PRACTICES.

It's critical to keep up with the most recent trends and best practices in the rapidly evolving world of Internet sales. This chapter will look at several ways to stay current and keep enhancing your internet sales tactics.

Following Industry Thought Leaders

Following thinking leaders in your business is one way to remain informed. These people frequently have a wealth of knowledge in their area of expertise, making them a good resource for information on current trends and best practices. To keep updated, read their blogs and articles, subscribe to their podcasts, and follow them on social media.

Participating in Online Communities and Forums

Another approach to keeping informed and learning from people in the field is to take part in online communities and forums. Join online communities and discussion boards to meet other entrepreneurs and experts in your field. These groups can be a great source of suggestions, criticism, and encouragement.

Attending Conferences and Events

Another approach to staying current with the newest trends and best practices in your field is to go to conferences and events. Keynote speakers, panel discussions, and workshops are frequently included in these events and can offer insightful information and education. They also offer chances for networking and contact with other experts in your field.

Continuously Learning and Experimenting:

To stay ahead of the curve, it is crucial to continuously learn and explore. To find out what works best for your business, take online courses, study books and articles, and try out various techniques and methods. Keep an open mind to trying new things and modifying your tactics as necessary in light of what you discover.

Take into account the following advice to stay current with the newest trends and best practices:

- Set aside time each week for your professional growth and learning.

- Participate in online forums and communities where you can meet people in your business.
- Go to conferences and events to keep up with current affairs and meet new people.
- Try out many different strategies and methods to evaluate which ones are most effective for your company.

You can continue to enhance and expand your online sales by keeping up with the most recent trends and best practices. Maintain your curiosity, remain open to learning, and be eager to try new things.

Appendix A: Tools and Resources for Online Sales

This appendix provides a list of tools and resources that can help you with various aspects of your online sales business.

E-commerce Platforms:
- Shopify
- WooCommerce
- BigCommerce
- Magento

Website and Design Tools:
- Wix
- Squarespace
- WordPress
- Canva

Payment Processors:
- PayPal
- Stripe
- Square
- Authorize.net

Shipping and Fulfillment:
- ShipStation
- Shippo
- FedEx
- UPS

Marketing and Advertising:
- Google Ads
- Facebook Ads
- Instagram Ads
- Mailchimp

Analytics and Data:
- Google Analytics
- Hotjar
- Crazy Egg
- SEMrush

Customer Service and Support:

- Zendesk
- Freshdesk
- Intercom
- Help Scout

Appendix B: Glossary of E-commerce Terms

This appendix provides a glossary of e-commerce terms to help you understand key concepts and terminology in the world of online sales.

- **E-commerce:** The buying and selling of goods and services online.

- **Online Store**: a website where customers can browse and purchase products and services.

- **Shopping Cart:** a software application that allows customers to select and purchase products online

- **Payment Gateway**: a software application that processes online payments.

- **Fulfilment**: The process of preparing and shipping orders to customers.

- **SEO**: Search Engine Optimization - the process of optimizing a website to improve its ranking in search engine results.

- **PPC**: Pay-Per-Click - a

model of online advertising where advertisers pay each time a user clicks on one of their ads.

- **Conversion Rate**: The percentage of website visitors who take a desired action, such as making a purchase.

- **A/B Testing**: The process of testing two versions of a website or marketing campaign to determine which performs better.

- **CRM**: Customer Relationship Management - the process of managing interactions with customers to improve relationships and increase sales.

- **Dropshipping**: a business model where the retailer does not hold inventory but instead relies on a supplier to fulfil orders directly to customers.

- **Affiliate Marketing**: a marketing strategy where businesses pay commissions to other websites or individuals for promoting their products or services.

- **ROI**: Return on Investment - a measure of the profitability of an investment, calculated as the ratio of the net profit to the investment cost.